Batch   5 Jan 20

(2) - Blueberries
            - Standard recipe
            - full measures
1.2kg frozen ~~~~~~
~~~~~~~~~~~~~
(~~~~)

Batch

(3) - Blue berries   800g
     - Standard recipe   Blueberries
                         FROZEN
     - Fruit not removed
     - ~~~~~~
     - straight into demijohn
     - skins NOT removed
     after 3 days
     - half recommended sugar
     added at 3 days gone.

     Sugar - 0.4kg on first day
            0.45 kg (½ raspberry
                     ½ lemon)
                skins   normal
     - fruit removed 2 Aug 20   3 day 1.
     - bottled 5 Sep 1 cup Suga added

12 Aug 20

Batch 4 — Gooseberries
- approx 1.8 kg of gooseberries
- 400g sugar. normal recipe
- Frozen.

• Remove fruit 8 Aug
- add $\frac{1}{2}$ (450 grams
                 sugar)

- chk to 5 am 25 Aug
- Bottled 5 Sep 20

Printed in Great
Britain
by Amazon

32400633R10071